The 25 Rules to Learn

About the Book

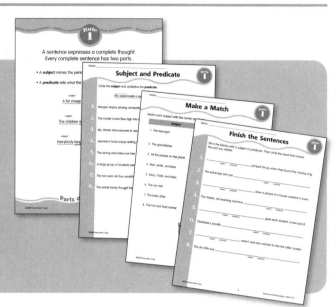

Grammar & Punctuation includes:

25 Rule Charts
Use the charts to introduce the rules. Animated versions of the charts are available as a bonus download. (See below.) Choose the rules and the order of use that is appropriate to your students' needs.

Student Practice Pages
Each rule is supported by 3 scaffolded, reproducible practice pages. Use the level that is appropriate for your students. The pages may be used with the whole class or as independent practice. They are also useful as homework review.

Downloadable Bonuses:

25 Rule Charts
These colorful, animated charts really focus students' attention on the rules introduced in this book. It's never been more fun to practice grammar and punctuation! To present a whole-class lesson, download the charts and connect your computer to a projection system. As a part of center time, students may view charts on classroom computers as they complete one of the practice activities.

Assessment
This 3-page assessment document provides a means of evaluating your students' acquisition of the grammar and punctuation rules presented. Download the pages and use them to monitor your students' progress.

Student Record Sheet
The student record sheet lists the 25 skills presented in this book. Download it to help you track your students' progress.

Student Handbook
Download and reproduce the handbook for each student. The 25 rules are shown, with room for students to write their own examples.

1. Click the *Choose a Rule* button to display the list of rules.

2. Click on a rule and it will be displayed.

3. Click on the arrow button. Rule explanations and examples will be displayed.

4. When you're finished, click on **List of Rules** to go back to the rules list or click on **Main Menu** to go back to the main menu.

How to Access the Downloadable Bonuses:

1. Go to evan-moor.com/resources.
2. Enter in your e-mail address and resource code for this product—EMC2713.
   Important: You **must** provide a valid e-mail address to access the content.
3. You will receive an e-mail with a link to the downloadable bonuses.
4. Download the bonuses and follow the instructions in the readme.txt file included with the install package.

A sentence expresses a complete thought.
Every complete sentence has two parts.

- A **subject** names the person, place, or thing the sentence is about.

- A **predicate** tells what the subject is or does.

subject	predicate
A fat sheep	ate grass in the field.

subject	predicate
The children	were playing dodge ball.

subject	predicate
Everybody	laughed at the clown's tricks.

Parts of a Sentence

Subject and Predicate

Rule 1

Circle the **subject** and underline the **predicate**.

(My sister) made a peanut butter and jelly sandwich.

1. Morgan enjoys playing computer games.

2. The model rocket flew high into the sky.

3. Ms. Winter told everyone to use their best penmanship.

4. Jasmine's horse enjoys eating carrots.

5. The strong wind blew our tree over.

6. A large group of students went to the movies.

7. The two-year-old boy wouldn't stop crying in the store.

8. The whole family thought the museum was awesome.

Make a Match

Match each subject with the correct predicate.

Subject	Predicate
1. The teenager	smiled when his grandson walked for the first time.
2. The grandfather	enjoyed talking on the telephone.
3. All the people on the plane	were the three students in the library.
4. Red, white, and blue	was eight hours long.
5. Mary, Todd, and Koko	were served a delicious lunch.
6. The car ride	are the colors of the flag.
7. The baby sitter	was glad to have a drink of water.
8. The hot and tired runner	was paid five dollars for watching the little boy.

Name _____

Finish the Sentences

Fill in the blanks with a subject or predicate. Then circle the word that names
the part you added.

1. _____ jumped for joy when they found the missing ring.
              subject   predicate

2. The extremely tall man _____.
                               subject   predicate

3. _____ drew a picture of a house covered in snow.
              subject   predicate

4. The rickety, old washing machine _____.
                                   subject   predicate

5. _____ gave each student a new pencil.
                subject   predicate

6. Penelope's poodle _____.
                        subject   predicate

7. _____ wasn't sure she wanted to ride the roller coaster.
              subject   predicate

8. The shy little boy _____.
                      subject   predicate

There are four kinds of sentences.
Each kind uses a specific ending punctuation.

- A **statement** tells something. It ends with a period (.).

    That is my new bicycle.

    I got it for my birthday.

- A **question** asks something. It ends with a question mark (**?**).

    Do you own a bicycle**?**

    Would you like to ride mine**?**

- A **command** tells someone to do something.* It ends with a period (.) *or an exclamation point (!)*

    Don't ride in the middle of the street.

    Stay close to the curb.

- An **exclamation** shows strong feeling. It ends with an exclamation mark (**!**).

    Look out for that truck**!** *(also a command)*

    That was a close call**!**

*See Notes to the Teacher on page 103 for additional information.

Kinds of Sentences

What Type of Sentence Is It?

Tell whether each sentence is a **statement**, **question**, **command**, or **exclamation**.

1. I'm excited to see the moons of Saturn through my telescope! _____

2. The moons of Saturn can be seen through a telescope. _____

3. What are the names of Saturn's moons? _____

4. Titan is one of the moons of Saturn. _____

5. Write a report about Titan. _____

6. Does Titan have an atmosphere? _____

7. Stop bumping my telescope! _____

8. I have learned many facts about the moons of Saturn. _____

Name It! Punctuate It!

Rule 2

Add the correct ending punctuation. Use **.**, **?**, or **!**. Then circle what each sentence is.

1. A piano has 88 keys ____.____

(statement) command
question exclamation

2. May I play the piano _____

statement command
question exclamation

3. Stop banging on the piano _____

statement command
question exclamation

4. Practice playing the piano for the next 30 minutes _____

statement command
question exclamation

5. Name three famous piano players _____

statement command
question exclamation

6. Who is your favorite piano player _____

statement command
question exclamation

7. I like playing the piano _____

statement command
question exclamation

8. Oh dear, the lid of the piano smashed my finger _____

statement command
question exclamation

Write It a New Way

Follow the directions to rewrite each sentence.

Bees collect pollen to make honey.

Make it a **question**.

Why do bees collect pollen?

1. Bees build their homes out of wax.

Make it a **question**.

_____

2. Did the bee sting you?

Make it an **exclamation**.

_____

3. The beekeeper collects honey from the hive.

Make it a **command**.

_____

4. Do you have a lot of bees in your garden?

Make it a **statement**.

_____

Conjunctions such as **and**, **or**, and **but** are used to join words or groups of words.

It's raining cats **and** dogs outside.

Do you want milk **or** orange juice?

I want to play, **but** I have work to do.

Conjunctions

Find the Conjunctions

Circle the conjunction in each sentence.

1. Students in Mr. Past's class were studying pilgrims and pioneers.

2. Do you want to write a story or a report?

3. I will write a story, but it won't be funny.

4. Everyone should eat more fruits and vegetables.

5. Do you like fruits or vegetables?

6. I like fruits, but I don't like vegetables.

7. Which type of music do you like best, jazz or rock?

8. I like jazz and rock.

9. I like jazz, but I don't like rock.

Add a Conjunction

Write the correct conjunction in each blank.

1. I'm on two teams, a soccer team _____ a baseball team.

2. I'm not sure which is more fun, being on a soccer team _____ a baseball team.

3. I will be on a soccer team, _____ not a baseball team.

4. Which do you want to see first, the monkeys _____ the bears?

5. You can find monkeys _____ bears at a zoo.

6. The monkeys moved around a lot, _____ the bears just stayed in one place.

7. Learning about the solar system is both fun _____ educational.

8. Do you want to learn about planets _____ moons?

9. My report is about planets, _____ not moons.

Use Conjunctions

A Write three sentences about **dogs**. Each sentence should use a different conjunction: **and**, **or**, and **but**.

1. _____

_____

2. _____

_____

3. _____

_____

B Write three sentences about **recess**. Each sentence should use a different conjunction: **and**, **or**, and **but**.

1. _____

_____

2. _____

_____

3. _____

_____

Nouns name a person, place, or thing. Some nouns name specific people, places, or things.

- **Common nouns** name any person, place, or thing. They do not begin with a capital letter.

- **Proper nouns** name a specific person, place, or thing. They begin with a capital letter.

common	proper
man	Mr. Jackson
amusement park	Disneyland
automobile	Cadillac
toy	Legos®
city	Boston

Common & Proper Nouns

Common and Proper Nouns

Rule
4

Label each noun as a **person**, **place**, or **thing**. Then tell whether it is **proper** or **common**.

	airport	place	common
1.	Mr. Banks		
2.	library		
3.	girl		
4.	Colorado		
5.	trumpet		
6.	Robby Robot		
7.	teacher		
8.	Krispy Donuts		

Name _____

Find the Proper Nouns

Cross out any letter that should be a capital letter. Then write the capital letter above it.

1. M̶ount E̶verest

2. mountain

3. yellowstone national park

4. main street

5. mr. nelson

6. cousin

7. ice cream

8. elisa's fine ice cream

9. grand canyon

10. lake superior

11. city

12. song

13. texas

14. computer

15. aunt helen

16. desk

Capital Letters

Copy the sentences. Use capital letters where needed.

1. my friend sarafina moved to santa fe, new mexico.

_____

_____

2. carrie said, "i want to go to uncle fred's for thanksgiving."

_____

_____

3. our minister, rev. murphy, has worked in churches in australia, guatemala, and california.

_____

_____

4. prof. j. e. evans and dr. james r. wilson were both born on january 6.

_____

_____

5. mother and her german friend, helga, want to go to a chinese restaurant for dinner.

_____

_____

Rule 5

Some nouns name only one person, place, or thing. Other nouns name more than one.

- **Singular nouns** name one person, place, or thing.

- **Plural nouns** name more than one.

singular	plural
cake	cakes
monkey	monkeys
man	men
box	boxes
bench	benches
puppy	puppies

Singular & Plural Nouns

Singular or Plural?

Write the letter **S** next to the singular nouns and **P** next to the plural nouns.

1. dog _____

2. dogs _____

3. mouse _____

4. mice _____

5. radios _____

6. radio _____

7. potato _____

8. potatoes _____

9. children _____

10. child _____

11. babies _____

12. baby _____

13. woman _____

14. women _____

15. house _____

16. houses _____

1 mouse

2 mice

Name _____

Make a Match

Draw a line from each singular noun to its plural.

chair	turkeys
man	geese
kangaroo	kangaroos
turkey	chairs
goose	men
dish	videos
picture	dishes
video	pictures

1 kangaroo   2 kangaroos

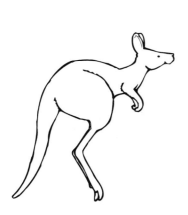
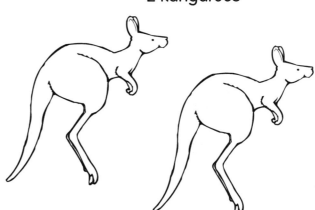

One or More Than One?

Write the correct word in each sentence.

1. The _____ were sitting in their seats quietly.

student   students

2. The girl's _____ were tired after running a mile.

foot   feet

3. The group had two _____ and one _____.

trumpet   trumpets   trombone   trombones

4. I need a _____ of sugar and two _____ of flour.

cup   cups   cup   cups

5. My dentist said I should brush all my _____ every day.

tooth   teeth

6. I saw a horse and two _____ in the field.

cow   cows

7. There were many _____ on the road.

car   cars

8. I ate a _____ for lunch.

hamburger   hamburgers

Rule 6

To make plural nouns, add **s** or **es**.

- For most nouns—add **s**.

    clock**s**   boat**s**   finger**s**

- For nouns ending in **s**, **sh**, **ch**, **x**, or **z**—add **es**.

    peach**es**   watch**es**   fox**es**

- For nouns ending in a consonant followed by **y**— change the **y** to **i** and add **es**.

    bab**ies**   cherr**ies**   berr**ies**

Forming Plural Nouns

More Than One

Write the plural for each noun. Add **s** or **es**.

1. table   _____

2. rug   _____

3. church   _____

4. computer   _____

5. flower   _____

6. dish   _____

7. school   _____

8. waltz   _____

9. tax   _____

10. lamp   _____

11. bus   _____

12. bush   _____

13. name   _____

14. fox   _____

15. plant   _____

16. cross   _____

Which Ending?

Write the plural for each noun. Add **s** or change the **y** to **i** and add **es**.

1. butterfly _____

2. penny _____

3. day _____

4. valley _____

5. body _____

6. lady _____

7. canary _____

8. posy _____

9. reply _____

10. copy _____

11. tray _____

12. library _____

13. turkey _____

14. city _____

15. berry _____

16. bunny _____

Name _____

Write the Plural

Write the plural noun in each blank.

1. Both of the _____ enjoy fishing.

girl

2. All of the _____ enjoy hiking.

boy

3. How many _____ can fit in the corral?

horse

4. _____ are on sale at the grocery store.

Cherry

5. There are some _____ on the bookshelf.

dictionary

6. There are ten _____ in a dime.

penny

7. How many _____ do you need for art class?

brush

8. There are two _____ in that cave.

fox

Rule 7

Some nouns have special plural forms.
These are called irregular plurals.

singular	plural
woman	women
man	men
child	children
foot	feet
mouse	mice
goose	geese
tooth	teeth
die	dice

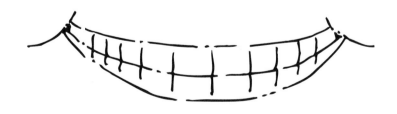

Irregular Plural Nouns

Name _____

Find the Plural

Rule 7

Circle the plural form of each noun.

1. men   man

2. goose   geese

3. calf   calves

4. mice   mouse

5. woman   women

6. child   children

7. teeth   tooth

8. feet   foot

9. ox   oxen

10. loaves   loaf

11. fireman   firemen

12. wives   wife

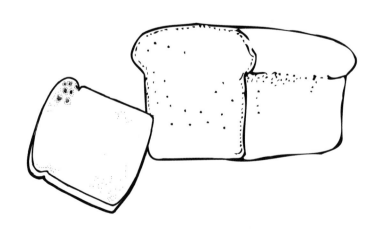

Is It Plural?

Write the correct word in the blank.

1. There is a group of _____ sitting at the table.
<small>woman   women</small>

2. I have three _____ missing.
<small>tooth   teeth</small>

3. My teacher has a bag of _____ for math time.
<small>die   dice</small>

4. How many _____ are in that car?
<small>policeman   policemen</small>

5. The _____ was playing with a stuffed bear.
<small>child   children</small>

6. I would like to buy a _____ for a pet.
<small>mouse   mice</small>

7. That _____ is my coach.
<small>man   men</small>

8. There were five _____ on the lake.
<small>goose   geese</small>

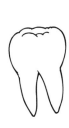

Write the Plural

Write the plural of each word. Then use the plural in a sentence.

1. child _____

_____

2. tooth _____

_____

3. mouse _____

_____

4. ox _____

_____

5. foot _____

_____

6. man _____

_____

8

A pronoun is a word that takes the place of one or more nouns.

in a subject	in a predicate
I	me
you	you
he	him
she	her
it	it
we	us
they	them

Kyle and Arnie rode bikes down the street.

They rode **them** down the street.

Alice fell down a rabbit hole.

She fell down **it**.

Carlos and I played with Maggie.

We played with **her**.

pronouns

Choose a Pronoun

Circle the pronoun that replaces the noun or nouns.

1. Mike   he   them   you

2. Eric and Kyle   it   I   them

3. Mandy   I   she   we

4. Ada and me   us   he   him

5. Mike and Mandy   me   they   it

6. Eric and I   he   they   we

7. mouse   it   me   they

8. mice   her   he   them

Write the Pronouns

Rewrite the sentences using pronouns for the underlined words.

1. <u>Adela</u> was planting <u>flowers</u> in the garden.

_____

2. <u>Adam</u> was helping <u>Adela</u> in the garden.

_____

3. <u>Adela</u> was watering <u>the garden</u>.

_____

4. <u>Adela and Adam</u> were pulling <u>weeds</u> out of the garden.

_____

5. <u>Adam</u> saw <u>a ladybug</u> on a leaf.

_____

Name _____

Cats and Dogs

Rule
8

Write the correct pronoun in each blank.

Yuki was so upset. _____ was walking her dog, Max,
                            Yuki

when a cat jumped in front of _____. Yuki screamed, and
                                   Yuki and Max

_____ began barking. The cat turned to hiss at _____.
      Max   Yuki and Max

This only made Max angry. _____ leaped toward the cat, pulling
                                 Max

the leash out of Yuki's hand. _____ watched _____
                                    Yuki   the cat and Max

run down the street. Luckily, Yuki's friend, Jill, saw what happened and

grabbed the leash. Yuki smiled as Jill handed _____
                                                    the leash

back to _____.
             Yuki

Name yourself last when you are talking about another person and yourself.

Jim and **I** play soccer.

The teacher and **I** worked the problem together.

Do you want to play with Jim and **me**?

Billy sits at the same table as Tanya and **me**.

To hear if you have used **I** and **me** correctly, leave the other person's name out. Which would you say?

Jim and **I** play soccer. **I** play soccer.	Jim and **me** play soccer. **Me** play soccer.
Give it to Frank and **me**. Give it to **me**.	Give it to Frank and **I**. Give it to **I**.

Using I & Me

I or Me?

Write **I** or **me** in each blank.

1. _____ went to the zoo with my family.

2. My sister and _____ enjoyed watching the monkeys.

3. My mom and _____ liked watching the elephants.

4. Our parents gave Sarah and _____ a bag of popcorn.

5. My sister gave _____ half of her sandwich.

6. _____ gave my sister half of my hot dog.

7. My dad gave my sister and _____ some money to buy dessert.

8. We enjoyed eating ice-cream cones, but _____ dripped some on my pants.

Name _____

An I and Me Story

Rule 9

Write **I** or **me** in each blank.

"Don't worry. Just make sure your life jacket is on tight," my

mother said to _____ right as _____ stepped into the canoe.

_____ checked my jacket, with one foot on shore and one foot in the

canoe. But the canoe wasn't planning to wait for _____. It began

to move into the lake. _____ lost my balance, and my mother grabbed

for _____. We both fell into the lake. My mother and _____

were happy that we were wearing our life jackets!

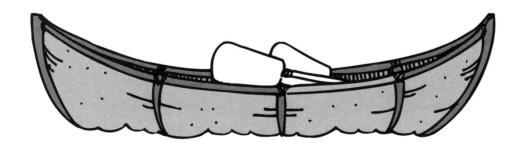

Name _____

Write a Story

Write a story about what you do at school. Use the words **I** and **me** in your story.

_____

_____

_____

_____

_____

_____

_____

Rule 10

A possessive noun tells who or what owns something.

- For **singular** nouns—add an apostrophe and **s** (**'s**).

  Kate**'s** old backpack

  Mrs. Smith**'s** class

  my sister**'s** tooth

  James**'s** book

- For **plural** nouns that end in **s**—add an apostrophe (**'**).

  the bees**'** hive

  the peaches**'** fuzz

  the babies**'** rattles

  the boys**'** clubhouse

- For **plural** nouns that do not end in **s**—add an apostrophe and **s** (**'s**).

  the men**'s** jackets

  the geese**'s** nests

  the children**'s** classroom

Forming Possessive Nouns

It's Yours

Write the possessive form of each noun.

1. This is my _____ hat.

brother

2. Follow the _____ tracks.

animal

3. Here is the _____ bottle.

baby

4. Here are the _____ bottles.

babies

5. Did you see _____ rabbit?

Fred

6. My _____ coat is over there.

mother

7. The _____ toys are missing.

kittens

8. This is _____ paper.

Mark

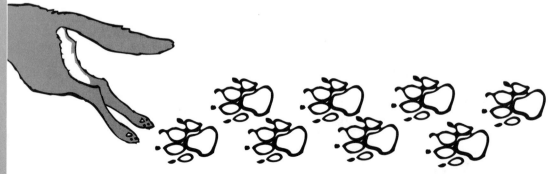

A Possessive Fish Tale

Write the possessive form in each blank.

Here is my _____ fish tank. This is my _____
family   brother

angel fish. This is my _____ guppy. This is my _____
sister   mother

neon. This is my _____ fantail. Phoebe, the baby of the
father

family, also owns a fish. _____ fish is plastic. This is because
Phoebe

Phoebe always wants to hold her fish. Everyone in my family likes their fish.

This includes Phoebe, even if _____ fish doesn't move much.
Phoebe

Name _____

Write Your Own Story

Write a story about your family and the things they own. Underline the possessive nouns in your story.

Rule 11

Possessive pronouns tell who or what owns something. They replace possessive nouns.

- Some possessive pronouns are used before a noun.

| my | your | his | her | its | our | their |

our home   **her** brother   **my** best friend

- Other possessive pronouns stand alone.

| mine | yours | his | hers | its | ours | theirs |

Is this book **yours**?   Yes, it is **mine**.

Possessive Pronouns

Name _____

Choose a Possessive Pronoun

Rule 11

Rewrite the sentences using a possessive pronoun for the underlined words.

| my | his | her | its | our | their |

1. I'm going to <u>Elisa's</u> house.

_____

2. This is <u>Ian's</u> guitar.

_____

3. Did you see <u>Elisa and Ian's</u> puppy?

_____

4. This is _____'s pencil. (Write your name in the blank.)

_____

5. Look at <u>the butterfly's</u> wings.

_____

6. This is <u>my family's</u> car.

_____

Write a Possessive Pronoun

Write a possessive pronoun in each blank for the underlined words.

mine	yours	theirs	his	hers	ours

1. The bike belongs to <u>Sarah</u>. The bike is _____.

2. The baseball belongs to <u>Mike</u>. The baseball is _____.

3. The skateboard belongs to <u>him</u>. The skateboard is _____.

4. The car belongs to <u>George and Sharon</u>. The car is _____.

5. The cat belongs to <u>me</u>. The cat is _____.

6. The swings belong to <u>us</u>. The swings are _____.

7. The telephone belongs to <u>you</u>. The telephone is _____.

8. The house belongs to <u>them</u>. The house is _____.

Find the Possessive Pronouns

Rule
11

Circle the possessive pronouns.

1. His friends are coming to the party.

2. There are balloons in our house.

3. Is that red hat hers?

4. My family will be there at noon.

5. That piece of cake is mine.

6. Those prizes are theirs.

7. Your cousin will get to play games.

8. That present is yours.

A verb tells what is happening to the noun.

- **Action verbs** show an action.

    My dog **ran** away.

    She **went** home after school.

- **Linking verbs** connect the subject to a noun or an adjective that describes it. The most commonly used linking verbs are **am**, **is**, **are**, **was**, and **were**.

    His sister **is** the trumpet player.

    The clowns **were** funny.

- **Helping verbs** come before the main verb to tell about the action. Some helping verbs are **will**, **has**, **had**, **have**, **could**, **would**, **should**, **do**, **does**, and **did**.

    I **will call** you later.

    She **has been** camping for a week.

    You **should read** that story.

    The astronauts **did land** on the moon.

Verbs

Action Verbs

Write an action verb in each blank.

1. The students _____ to the playground.

2. The horse _____ over the fence.

3. Pam _____ a picture.

4. The worm _____ on the ground.

5. Lee _____ a model rocket into the sky.

6. She _____ a story about herself.

7. He _____ a dime on the sidewalk.

8. They _____ during recess.

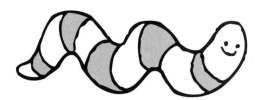

Which Linking Verb?

Write the correct linking verb in each blank.

1. William _____ the first person to cross the finish line.
_{was   are   were}

2. William said, "I _____ proud of the way I ran."
_{are   am   were}

3. Ben and Lexi _____ the second and third people to cross the finish line.
_{was   were   is}

4. They said, "We _____ proud of the way we ran."
_{am   is   are}

5. Leo _____ the last person to cross the finish line.
_{were   are   was}

6. He said, "I _____ last, but I _____ also proud of the way I ran."
_{are   was   is}   _{am   is   were}

7. Leo continued, "This _____ the first time I ever finished a race!"
_{am   were   was}

8. William, Ben, and Lexi _____ all proud of Leo.
_{is   was   were}

Choose the Helping Verb

Write the correct helping verb in each blank.

1. May and Ray asked if they _____ play a game of checkers.

could   do   has

2. Their mother wasn't sure they _____ play the game.

has   have   should

3. She asked if they _____ made their beds.

has   had   do

4. May and Ray said, "We _____ make our beds right away."

will   has   does

5. After they _____ made their beds, they played the game.

will   had   did

6. Ray and May said, "If we could, we _____ play checkers all day."

did   would   have

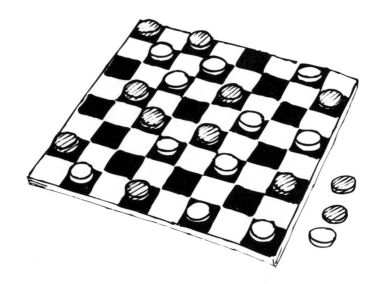

The verb in a sentence must agree with the subject of the sentence.

- If the <u>subject</u> is singular, the **verb** must be singular.

  Our <u>apple tree</u> **blooms** in April.

  <u>Mark</u> **is playing** basketball after school.

  An <u>airplane</u> **flies** high above the ground.

- If the <u>subject</u> is plural, the **verb** must be plural.

  Most <u>apple trees</u> **bloom** in April.

  <u>We</u> **are playing** basketball after school.

  <u>Airplanes</u> **fly** high above the ground.

Subject-Verb Agreement

Find Agreement

Circle the correct verb.

1. Monica **is/are**

2. balloons **floats/float**

3. puppies **is/are**

4. ball **bounces/bounce**

5. Fred and Fay **walks/walk**

6. LeeAnn **lifts/lift**

7. penguin **stays/stay**

8. flowers **smells/smell**

9. mouse **moves/move**

10. Stan **stamps/stamp**

11. Gerry, Jill, and Janet **gathers/gather**

12. frog **dives/dive**

13. watermelon **ripens/ripen**

14. students **learns/learn**

15. eggs **cooks/cook**

16. camera **takes/take**

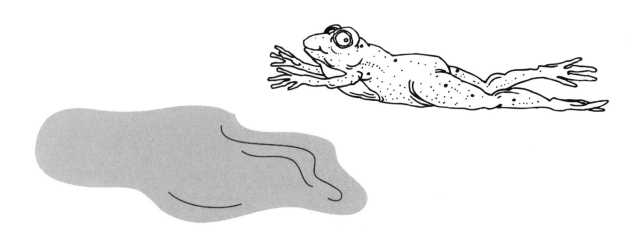

Write a Word

Write the correct verb in each blank.

1. The crayons _____ on the floor.
<small>is   are</small>

2. The crayons _____ in the box.
<small>was   were</small>

3. Tara _____ pictures every day.
<small>draws   draw</small>

4. Tom and Teri _____ pictures, too.
<small>draws   draw</small>

5. Chad _____ flowers from the garden.
<small>pick   picks</small>

6. Allen and Bob _____ flowers, too.
<small>pick   picks</small>

7. The flowers _____ in a vase.
<small>is   are</small>

8. The flowers _____ on the table.
<small>was   were</small>

Agreeable Writing

A Write three sentences with **singular** nouns.

1. _____

_____

2. _____

_____

3. _____

_____

B Write three sentences with **plural** nouns.

1. _____

_____

2. _____

_____

3. _____

_____

The tense of a verb tells when an action occurs.

- **present**—the action is happening now.

    I **am eating** peanut butter and toast for breakfast.

- **past**—the action already happened.

    I **ate** cereal with bananas for breakfast yesterday.

- **future**—the action is going to happen.

    Tomorrow I **will eat** eggs and bacon.

Verb Tenses

Pick the Tense

Write **present**, **past**, or **future** for each sentence.

1. Frank will fly his kite tomorrow.   _____

2. Penny is outside flying her kite.   _____

3. Pat flew her kite yesterday.   _____

4. Learn this new dance step with me.   _____

5. We will learn the new dance step later.   _____

6. We learned that dance step already.   _____

7. I am cooking hamburgers.   _____

8. I will cook the hamburgers in 20 minutes.   _____

9. The hamburgers were cooked 20 minutes ago.   _____

Rewrite the Tense

A Rewrite this sentence in the **present** tense and **past** tense.

Greg will paint a picture in art class.

1. _____

2. _____

B Rewrite this sentence in the **present** tense and **future** tense.

Ann worked at a restaurant.

1. _____

2. _____

C Rewrite this sentence in the **future** tense and **past** tense.

Hayden is mailing a letter.

1. _____

2. _____

Name _____

Write a Past Tense Story

Rule
14

Write a story about something you did yesterday. Use verbs in the **past** tense.

_____

_____

_____

_____

_____

_____

_____

Rule 15

Use the rules below for present tense verbs when the subject is singular.

- For most verbs—add **s**.

| sit**s** | look**s** | sing**s** | play**s** |

She **sits** and **looks** at books.

Linda **sings** songs when she **plays** with her dolls.

- For verbs that end in **s**, **sh**, **ch**, **x**, or **z**—add **es**.

| pitch**es** | wash**es** | catch**es** | watch**es** |

Bob **pitches** the ball to Tina.

She **catches** it.

- For verbs ending in a consonant followed by a **y**—change the **y** to **i** and add **es**.

| carr**ies** | bur**ies** | hurr**ies** | marr**ies** |

My dog, Zip, **hurries** to the backyard.

He **buries** his bone under a bush.

Forming Present Tense Verbs

Add s or es

Write the present tense for each verb.

1. dash _____

2. sleep _____

3. itch _____

4. fix _____

5. crawl _____

6. send _____

7. launch _____

8. stretch _____

9. fizz _____

10. rush _____

11. mix _____

12. wait _____

13. attach _____

14. push _____

15. laugh _____

16. look _____

In the Present

Write the present tense for each verb.

1. cry _____

2. gather _____

3. tip _____

4. slip _____

5. dry _____

6. pluck _____

7. race _____

8. step _____

9. rub _____

10. pick _____

11. copy _____

12. perform _____

13. reply _____

14. study _____

15. wander _____

16. enjoy _____

 Grammar and Punctuation • EMC 2713

An Agreeable Math Story

Write the present tense for each verb.

1. Rita _____ to George Washington Elementary School.
walk

2. She _____ her school and _____ hard.
like · study

3. Rita never _____ through her math homework.
rush

4. She _____ working with numbers is fun.
believe

5. Rita _____ she can always find the answer.
think

6. Rita _____ she can go to summer math camp.
hope

7. Her mom _____ her to go.
want

8. Rita _____ to learn new things at math camp.
plan

Add **ed** to make the past tense of most verbs.

- For most verbs—just add **ed**.

    pitch**ed**   paint**ed**   walk**ed**

- For verbs ending with a silent **e**—drop the **e** and add **ed**.

    danc**ed**   rac**ed**   bak**ed**

- For verbs ending in a consonant followed by a **y**—
  change the **y** to **i** and add **ed**.

    hurr**ied**   carr**ied**   bur**ied**

- Some verbs have an **irregular** past tense.

    dig—**dug**   catch—**caught**   sleep—**slept**

    eat—**ate**   buy—**bought**   write—**wrote**

    run—**ran**   sing—**sang**   ride—**rode**

Forming Past Tense Verbs

In the Past

Write the past tense for these verbs.

1. dash _____

2. move _____

3. live _____

4. fix _____

5. crawl _____

6. use _____

7. care _____

8. stretch _____

9. fizz _____

10. tape _____

11. mix _____

12. wait _____

13. bake _____

14. push _____

15. laugh _____

16. look _____

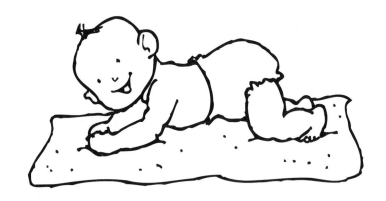

Past Tense Verbs

Write the past tense for these verbs.

1. cry _____

2. gather _____

3. walk _____

4. pace _____

5. dry _____

6. pluck _____

7. race _____

8. save _____

9. listen _____

10. pick _____

11. copy _____

12. fry _____

13. reply _____

14. enjoy _____

15. wander _____

16. study _____

Irregular Past Tense

Circle the irregular past tense verbs.

1. begin   began

2. threw   throw

3. take   took

4. saw   see

5. ring   rang

6. knew   know

7. hid   hide

8. go   went

9. gave   give

10. fall   fell

11. ate   eat

12. draw   drew

13. do   did

14. came   come

15. broke   break

16. hold   held

Adjectives are words that describe nouns or pronouns.

An adjective can tell three things:

- **what kind**

    A **furry** monkey climbed a **tall** tree.

    The **sleek**, **shiny** jet roared into the **cloudy** sky.

- **which one**

    That purple bicycle is mine.

    The **second** boy in line is my brother.

- **how many**

    Several children took part in the race.

    There are **six** cookies to divide among the **three** children.

Adjectives

67

What Kind?

Write a different adjective in each blank.

Have you seen that _____ bird with _____

feathers on its head, a _____ beak, and _____ legs? That

_____ bird darts in and out of the _____ bird feeder.

When there is a _____ noise, he doesn't fly away. But when there

is a _____ rain, he hides in our mailbox. I hope you will be able to

see this _____ bird someday.

Which One?

A Read the story.

> The finish line was in sight. Abby crossed the finish line before
>
> anyone else. She was happy to win but also wanted to be a good sport.
>
> So she cheered for the other runners as they crossed the finish line in this
>
> order: Betty, Cathy, Dede, Eva, Flo, Gail, Heather, Ishi, and Jill.

B Fill in the blanks to tell who came in first through tenth.

Abby was the _____ to cross the finish line.

Betty came in _____. Cathy was _____.

Dede was happy being _____. The person to come in

_____ was Eva. Flo came in _____. The

_____ person was Gail. Heather's all-time best was to

finish _____. Ishi finished _____.

Finally, Jill came in _____.

How Many?

A Circle the words that tell **how many**.

1. Those six boys visited several friends.

2. We have a dozen cookies for a few children.

3. A couple of friends collected many baseball cards.

4. This small group of people has a million ideas.

5. There was one adult for every five students on the bus.

6. Three students read all of the poems to the class.

B Write a word that tells **how many** in each of the blanks.

1. _____ girls talked for _____ hours on the telephone.

2. There are _____ balls for _____ children.

3. _____ friends played for _____ days.

4. Are those _____ toys for your _____ pets?

5. We have _____ hats for _____ players.

6. She poured _____ gallons of water into _____ different fish tanks.

Adjectives can make comparisons.

- Use **er** to compare two people, places, or things.

  Sally is **younger** than Ken.

  This book is **thicker** than that book.

  I want the **bigger** of the two balloons.

  A hummingbird is **smaller** than a pigeon.

- Use **est** to compare three or more people, places, or things.

  She is the **youngest** child in her family.

  This is the **thickest** book on the shelf.

  The **biggest** balloon in the bunch floated away.

  Hummingbirds are the **smallest** birds on Earth.

Comparative & Superlative Adjectives

Two or More?

Write the correct adjective in the blanks.

1. Ben had a _____ ice-cream cone than Brian.
bigger   biggest

2. Their father had the _____ ice-cream cone.
bigger   biggest

3. Shelley is _____ than Sue. Sue is _____ than Shelley.
taller   tallest   shorter   shortest

4. Shelley is the _____ girl in the class.
taller   tallest

5. It was _____ on Monday than on Wednesday.
hotter   hottest

6. Friday was the _____ day of the week.
hotter   hottest

7. Odie's dog is the _____ in the neighborhood.
older   oldest

8. Odie's dog is _____ than Olaf's dog.
older   oldest

Comparisons

Write one sentence comparing two people, places, or things. Write another sentence comparing three or more people, places, or things.

small

1. _____

2. _____

sweet

3. _____

4. _____

green

5. _____

6. _____

smooth

7. _____

8. _____

Name _____

The Hottest Day

Write a story using the adjectives in the box. Add **er** or **est** to the adjectives before using them in your story.

hot	yellow	warm	bright	great

Rule 19

The words **a**, **an**, and **the** are called articles.

I saw **a** boy.

Meg put **the** ball away.

You need **an** umbrella on **a** rainy day.

• Use **a** with words that begin with a consonant sound.

a box   **a** chair   **a** letter

• Use **an** with words that begin with a vowel sound.

an apple   **an** elephant   **an** insect

Articles

Name _____

Which Article?

Write **a**, **an**, or **the** in the blanks.

1. Mark wears _____ raincoat and takes _____ umbrella with him when it rains.

2. Did _____ cold weather bother you?

3. Tina ate _____ orange and _____ sandwich for lunch.

4. Don't forget to take _____ garbage out.

5. _____ elephant was marching in _____ parade.

6. Mother put _____ apple and _____ pear in _____ fruit salad.

7. Is _____ octopus _____ animal that lives in _____ sea?

8. I saw _____ chimpanzee, _____ gorilla, and _____ orangutan

at _____ Primate Center.

A Picnic

Write a different word in each blank to complete the sentences.

1. We loaded our stuff into the _____.

2. We drove to the _____.

3. We took a _____ and an _____ out of the _____.

4. We ate a _____, a _____, and an _____.

5. We played with a _____ and an _____.

6. We went on a hike and saw a _____ and an _____.

7. We took a nap on a _____ under the _____.

8. Then we jumped into the _____ and drove home.

What fun!

Name _____

A or An?

A Explain when you use **a** and when you use **an** in front of a noun.

_____

_____

B Write a sentence with each of these words. Use **a** and **an** correctly.

igloo dragonfly onion apple parade

1. _____

_____

2. _____

_____

3. _____

_____

4. _____

_____

5. _____

_____

Rule 20

Commas are used to separate three or more words or phrases in a series.

I saw bears, giraffes, and kangaroos at the zoo.

We ate fried chicken, potato chips, and chocolate cake.

Dave jumped into the water, swam across the lake,
and pulled himself up onto the raft.

Comma Usage

Name _____

The Comma Connection

Rule 20

Add commas where they are needed in the sentences.

1. Mark Danielle and Greg may go to lunch first.

2. I need a pencil a notebook and an eraser for class.

3. Please go outside look for your brother and tell him to come home.

4. I have Creeping Buttercup Golden Aster Edelweiss and Cupid's Dart in my garden.

5. My favorite colors are red crimson magenta vermilion and pink.

6. Please stack the red block first the green block second and the blue block last.

7. You are the happiest funniest friendliest and kindest person I know.

8. We will warm up shoot baskets practice defense and play a game.

9. Cindy asked Glen Robin and Dan to her birthday party.

10. We learned about nouns verbs and pronouns in class.

Name _____

A Model

Add commas where they are needed in the story.

Andrea wanted to build a model airplane. She opened the box. She found instructions plastic parts and a page of decals. Her mother asked her to make a snack for her little sister. Andrea gave her sister some popcorn a banana and an apple. Andrea's mother asked her to do her homework.

She read for 20 minutes solved math problems and wrote in her journal.

Her mother told her that she was a "model" daughter.

Name _____

Use Commas

1. Write a sentence that tells three things you do to get ready for school.

_____

_____

2. Write a sentence that tells three things you do at school.

_____

_____

3. Write a sentence that lists three of your friends.

_____

_____

4. Write a sentence that lists your three favorite foods.

_____

_____

5. Write a sentence that lists three kinds of pets you would like to have.

_____

_____

Rule 21

Commas follow specific rules when used in dates and addresses.

- A **comma** is used to separate the day and year in a date.*

February 23, 2009

July 4, 1776

- A **comma** is used to separate a city and state, province, or country.*

Fresno, California

Vancouver, British Columbia

Paris, France

*See Notes to the Teacher on page 103 for additional information.

Comma Usage

A Time and Place for Commas

A Use commas to separate the day and year.

1. September 30 1994

2. January 1 2012

3. May 25 1801

4. November 19 1940

B Use commas to separate the city and state, province, or country.

1. Greeley Colorado

2. Surprise Arizona

3. New York New York

4. San Francisco California

5. Ottawa Ontario

6. Beijing China

Your Personal Commas

Write the answers to these questions. Remember to use commas correctly.

1. What is your birth date? Include the month, day, and year.

_____

2. Where do you live? Include the city and state.

_____

3. Where were you born? Include the city and state.

_____

4. What was the first day of school? Include the month, day, and year.

_____

5. What is the last day of school? Include the month, day, and year.

_____

Doug's Bugs

Rule 21

Add commas where they are needed in the story.

Doug was born on May 7 1996. He grew up in Richmond Virginia.

Doug first discovered bugs on April 4 2002. He was at a park in Denver

Colorado. Something red with black spots crawled onto his leg. Next, he

found a bug with two big eyes on July 16 2002. He found a shiny green

bug in Omaha Nebraska. He began collecting tiny bugs on July 11 2007.

He had more than 60 different tiny bugs by October 1 2008. Doug plans

to continue his bug studies next summer in Phoenix Arizona. He may

also travel to Juneau Alaska.

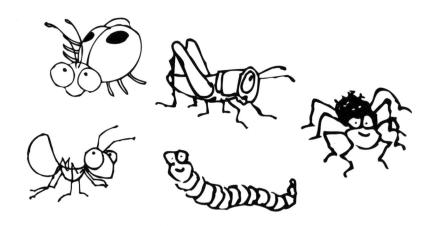

Rule 22

Commas follow specific rules when used after introductory words and to set off the name of the person being spoken to.

- A **comma** is used after introductory words such as **yes**, **no**, and **well**.

  Well, I guess you can go now.

  Yes, you may have a cookie.

  No, it's too late to watch television.

- A **comma** is used to set off the name of a person being spoken to from the rest of the sentence.

  Mary, is this your backpack?

  Come here, Tony, and clean up this mess.

  Mr. Ginsburg, the dentist is ready for you now.

Comma Usage

A Comma

Add commas to the sentences where they are needed.

1. Maranda did you remember to put a comma after your name?

2. Yes I remembered.

3. Here's a hard question Mary for you to answer.

4. Sure I'll try to answer the question.

5. Frank would you like to ride my skateboard?

6. Well the last time I rode your skateboard I hurt my knee, so no thanks.

7. Dad are we there yet?

8. No we just got in the car!

Use Commas

A Write two sentences where a comma is needed after an introductory word such as **yes**, **no**, or **well**.

1. _____

_____

2. _____

_____

B Write two sentences where a comma is needed to separate the name of a person being spoken to from the rest of the sentence.

1. _____

_____

2. _____

_____

A Hiking Story

Add commas to the story where they are needed.

September 4 2008 was a great day. I was on a hiking trail with my parents in Rocky Mountain National Park. The park is west of Estes Park Colorado. Most of the snow had melted, and many of the wildflowers were in bloom. We hiked on the trail. I saw a person who looked familiar. "Mike is that you?" I asked.

"Yes it's me," he replied.

"Wow it is great to see you!" I said. It was good to talk to my old friend again!

Rule 23

Commas follow specific rules when used in a friendly letter.

- A **comma** is used after the greeting.

Dear Grandmother,

Dear Paul,

Dear Uncle Teddy,

- A **comma** is used after the closing.

Love,

Your friend,

Sincerely,

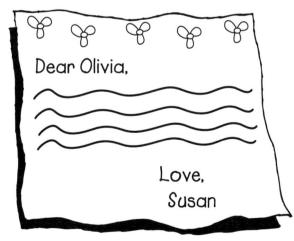

Dear Olivia,

Love,
Susan

Comma Usage

Add Commas

Add commas where they are needed.

Dear Principal Bond

   Thank you for reading to us yesterday. We enjoyed the way you sounded like a frog when you read. Come read to us again soon.

                              Sincerely

                              Ms. Writewell's Third-Grade Class

---

Dear Mr. Fixit

   Will you please fix my leaky roof? I was reading the newspaper at my kitchen table, and water from the ceiling dripped on my head! Thank you for taking care of this problem.

                              Sincerely

                              Mr. Allwet

Dear Principal Bond

   The members of the "Frog Imitators Club" are pleased to announce that you have won the "Best Frog Imitator" award. You will receive the award and a trip to the Lily Pad Resort.

                              Sincerely

                              President Frogg

Commas in a Letter

Add commas where they are needed.

Dear Aunt Edna

I'm learning how to use commas in the greeting and closing of

letters. I have learned how to use commas to separate phrases the day

and year and the city and state. Finally I have learned how to use commas

after an introductory word and after the name of a person. I've learned

a lot about commas.

Aunt Edna please write a letter to me soon. Here's my new address:

101 East Comma Place

Wichita Kansas

Your nephew

Edward

Letter Perfect

Write a letter to a friend. Tell your friend when to use commas.

_____

_____

_____

_____

_____

_____

_____

Rule 24

Quotation marks (" ") show the exact words of a speaker.

"Penguins cannot fly," explained the teacher.

"Do you know how to ski?" asked Mary Beth.

"That's funny!" laughed Sidney.

Quotation Marks

What Did You Say?

Rule
24

Add quotation marks where they are needed.

1. Was that our bus we just missed? asked Ms. Beatrice.

2. Paul yelled, Last one in the pool is a poodle!

3. This is my best doll, Dolores said proudly.

4. The little girl whined, I can't see the movie. The man in front of me is too tall.

5. Would you like to have a cookie? asked Mother.

6. Look what I found! A brand new penny! said Sarah excitedly.

7. Now I understand, said Sidney when he was able to solve the math problem.

8. May I have a drink of water? asked Wally.

A Quotable Story

Add quotation marks where they are needed.

Amy is my little sister. I brought her to the amusement park with me.

I want to ride the merry-go-round! shouted Amy. I want to ride

the zebra, she said.

OK! OK! You can ride the zebra, but then leave me alone, I told her.

Amy stood there looking into the glass eyes of the zebra. The zebra

doesn't like me, she said.

You're imagining things, I replied.

He hates me! Amy yelled back.

Get on that zebra now or we're leaving! I said. Amy started to cry.

I felt bad.

Amy, come sit on my lap while I ride the zebra, I suggested. Amy

jumped onto my lap. The music started, and away we went, galloping

around and around.

97

An Unusual Conversation

Give the two characters below a name. Then write what they might be saying to each other. Be sure to use quotation marks.

_____   _____

_____

_____

_____

_____

_____

_____

Rule 25

Use these rules when using the words **can** and **may**.

- Use **can** to tell that someone is able to do something.

- Use **may** to ask or give permission to do something.

The prince **can** sing beautifully.

May she sing in the talent show?

Can Alice cook?

Alice **may** cook if she wants to.

Word Usage

May or Can?

Write **may** or **can** in the blanks.

1. He _____ make popcorn in a microwave.

2. _____ I use the microwave?

3. We _____ use the watercolors without making a mess.

4. Mr. Pigment, _____ we use your watercolors?

5. Mr. Pigment said that we _____ use his watercolors whenever we want.

6. _____ I march in the parade?

7. Yes, you _____ march in the parade.

8. I _____ march for two hours, but then I'll need to rest.

9. Jake's sister _____ play the drums very well.

10. Jake _____ play the piano.

A May or Can Story

Rule 25

Write **may** or **can** in the blanks.

"_____ I help you?" asked the woman behind the counter.

"Yes, _____ I have a four-scoop sundae?" asked the little boy.

"You _____, but are you sure you _____ eat it all?"

"I _____," the little boy insisted.

"OK, I _____ make one for you in a minute," the woman said.

The little boy took the sundae and began eating. Three of the little boy's

friends peeked over the counter, each holding a spoon. When all the ice cream,

whipped cream, and cherries were eaten, the little boy smiled and said,

"See, I _____ eat it all. The more friends you have, the more ice cream

you _____ eat!"

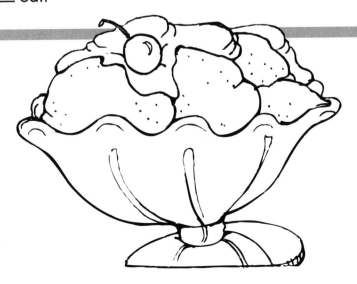

Grammar and Punctuation • EMC 2713

Name _____

Write a Story

Write a story about something you would like to do after school. Use the words **may** and **can** in your story.

_____

_____

_____

_____

_____

_____

_____

Notes to the Teacher

Rule 2, page 7

In an imperative sentence (one that gives a command), the subject *you* is understood.

Stop!

Walk on the sidewalk.

Pass the butter, please.

Rule 21, page 83

In running text, a comma follows as well as precedes both the year and the state, province, or country.

The events of April 18, 1775, have long been celebrated in song and story.

The electrical storms in Flagstaff, Arizona, are no less than spectacular.

Answer Key

Page 4
1. (Morgan) enjoys playing computer games.
2. (The model rocket) flew high into the sky.
3. (Ms. Winter) told everyone to use their best penmanship.
4. (Jasmine's horse) enjoys eating carrots.
5. (The strong wind) blew our tree over.
6. (A large group of students) went to the movies.
7. (The two-year-old boy) wouldn't stop crying in the store.
8. (The whole family) thought the museum was awesome.

Page 5
1. The teenager
   enjoyed talking on the telephone.
2. The grandfather
   smiled when his grandson walked for the first time.
3. All the people on the plane
   were served a delicious lunch.
4. Red, white, and blue
   are the colors of the flag.
5. Mary, Todd, and Koko
   were the three students in the library.
6. The car ride
   was eight hours long.
7. The baby sitter
   was paid five dollars for watching the little boy.
8. The hot and tired runner
   was glad to have a drink of water.

Page 6
Answers will vary.
1. subject
2. predicate
3. subject
4. predicate
5. subject
6. predicate
7. subject
8. predicate

Page 8
1. exclamation
2. statement
3. question
4. statement
5. command
6. question
7. exclamation
8. statement

Page 9
Answers may vary.
1. . statement
2. ? question
3. ! exclamation
4. . command
5. . command
6. ? question
7. . statement
8. ! exclamation

Page 10
Answers may vary.
1. Do bees build their homes out of wax?
2. That bee stung me!
3. Collect honey from the hive.
4. I have a lot of bees in my garden.

Page 12
1. and
2. or
3. but
4. and
5. or
6. but
7. or
8. and
9. but

Page 13
1. and
2. or
3. but
4. or
5. and
6. but
7. and
8. or OR and
9. but

Page 14

Answers will vary. Check for proper use of conjunctions.

Page 16

1. person, proper
2. place, common
3. person, common
4. place, proper
5. thing, common
6. thing, proper
7. person, common
8. thing, proper

Page 17

1. Mount Everest
3. Yellowstone National Park
4. Main Street
5. Mr. Nelson
8. Elisa's Fine Ice Cream
9. Grand Canyon
10. Lake Superior
13. Texas
15. Aunt Helen

Page 18

1. My, Sarafina, Santa Fe, New Mexico
2. Carrie, I, Uncle Fred's, Thanksgiving
3. Our, Rev. Murphy, Australia, Guatemala, California
4. Prof. J. E. Evans, Dr. James R. Wilson, January
5. Mother, German, Helga, Chinese

Page 20

1. S	9. P
2. P	10. S
3. S	11. P
4. P	12. S
5. P	13. S
6. S	14. P
7. S	15. S
8. P	16. P

Page 21

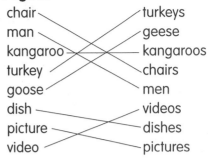

Page 22

1. students
2. feet
3. trumpets, trombone
4. cup, cups
5. teeth
6. cows
7. cars
8. hamburger

Page 24

1. tables	9. taxes
2. rugs	10. lamps
3. churches	11. buses
4. computers	12. bushes
5. flowers	13. names
6. dishes	14. foxes
7. schools	15. plants
8. waltzes	16. crosses

Page 25

1. butterflies	9. replies
2. pennies	10. copies
3. days	11. trays
4. valleys	12. libraries
5. bodies	13. turkeys
6. ladies	14. cities
7. canaries	15. berries
8. posies	16. bunnies

Page 26
1. girls
2. boys
3. horses
4. Cherries
5. dictionaries
6. pennies
7. brushes
8. foxes

Page 28
1. men
2. geese
3. calves
4. mice
5. women
6. children
7. teeth
8. feet
9. oxen
10. loaves
11. firemen
12. wives

Page 29
1. women
2. teeth
3. dice
4. policemen
5. child
6. mouse
7. man
8. geese

Page 30
Sentences will vary. Check for proper use of plural nouns.
1. children
2. teeth
3. mice
4. oxen
5. feet
6. men

Page 32
1. he
2. them
3. she
4. us
5. they
6. we
7. it
8. them

Page 33
1. She, them
2. He, her
3. She, it
4. They, them
5. He, it

Page 34
She, them, he, them, He, She, them, it, her

Page 36
1. I
2. I
3. I
4. me
5. me
6. I
7. me
8. I

Page 37
me, I, I, me, I, me, I

Page 38
Answers will vary. Check for proper use of *I* and *me.*

Page 40
1. brother's
2. animal's
3. baby's
4. babies'
5. Fred's
6. mother's
7. kittens'
8. Mark's

Page 41
family's, brother's, sister's, mother's, father's, Phoebe's, Phoebe's

Page 42
Answers will vary. Check for proper use of possessive nouns.

Page 44

1. her
2. his
3. their
4. my
5. its
6. our

Page 45

1. hers
2. his
3. his
4. theirs
5. mine
6. ours
7. yours
8. theirs

Page 46

1. His
2. our
3. hers
4. My
5. mine
6. theirs
7. Your
8. yours

Page 48

Answers will vary. Check for proper use of action verbs.

Page 49

1. was
2. am
3. were
4. are
5. was
6. was, am
7. was
8. were

Page 50

1. could
2. should
3. had
4. will
5. had
6. would

Page 52

1. is
2. float
3. are
4. bounces
5. walk
6. lifts
7. stays
8. smell
9. moves
10. stamps
11. gather
12. dives
13. ripens
14. learn
15. cook
16. takes

Page 53

1. are
2. were
3. draws
4. draw
5. picks
6. pick
7. are
8. were

Page 54

Answers will vary. Check for proper noun-verb agreement.

Page 56

1. future
2. present
3. past
4. present
5. future
6. past
7. present
8. future
9. past

Page 57

1. Greg is painting (OR paints) a picture in art class.
2. Greg painted a picture in art class.
3. Ann works (OR is working) at a restaurant.
4. Ann will work at a restaurant.
5. Hayden will mail a letter.
6. Hayden mailed a letter.

Page 58

Answers will vary. Check for proper use of past tense verbs.

Page 60

1. dashes	9. fizzes
2. sleeps	10. rushes
3. itches	11. mixes
4. fixes	12. waits
5. crawls	13. attaches
6. sends	14. pushes
7. launches	15. laughs
8. stretches	16. looks

Page 61

1. cries	9. rubs
2. gathers	10. picks
3. tips	11. copies
4. slips	12. performs
5. dries	13. replies
6. plucks	14. studies
7. races	15. wanders
8. steps	16. enjoys

Page 62

1. walks
2. likes, studies
3. rushes
4. believes
5. thinks
6. hopes
7. wants
8. plans

Page 64

1. dashed	9. fizzed
2. moved	10. taped
3. lived	11. mixed
4. fixed	12. waited
5. crawled	13. baked
6. used	14. pushed
7. cared	15. laughed
8. stretched	16. looked

Page 65

1. cried	9. listened
2. gathered	10. picked
3. walked	11. copied
4. paced	12. fried
5. dried	13. replied
6. plucked	14. enjoyed
7. raced	15. wandered
8. saved	16. studied

Page 66

1. began	9. gave
2. threw	10. fell
3. took	11. ate
4. saw	12. drew
5. rang	13. did
6. knew	14. came
7. hid	15. broke
8. went	16. held

Page 68

Answers will vary. Check for proper use of adjectives.

Page 69

first, second, third, fourth, fifth, sixth, seventh, eighth, ninth, tenth

Page 70

1. six, several
2. dozen, few
3. couple, many
4. small, million
5. one, five
6. three, all

Answers will vary. Check for proper use of adjectives that tell how many.

Page 72

1. bigger
2. biggest
3. taller, shorter
4. tallest
5. hotter
6. hottest
7. oldest
8. older

Page 73

Answers will vary. Check for proper use of comparative and superlative adjectives.

Page 74

Answers will vary. Check for proper use of comparative and superlative adjectives.

Page 76

1. a, an
2. the
3. an, a
4. the
5. An, the OR The, a
6. an, a, the
7. the, an, the OR an, an, the
8. a, a, an, the

Page 77

Answers will vary. Check for proper use of *a, an,* and *the*.

Page 78

Use *a* with words that begin with a consonant sound. Use *an* with words that begin with a vowel sound.

Answers will vary. Check for proper use of *a* and *an*.

Page 80

1. Mark, Danielle,
2. pencil, notebook,
3. outside, brother,
4. Buttercup, Aster, Edelweiss,
5. red, crimson, magenta, vermilion,
6. first, second,
7. happiest, funniest, friendliest,
8. up, baskets, defense,
9. Glen, Robin,
10. nouns, verbs,

Page 81

instructions, parts, popcorn, banana, minutes, problems,

Page 82

Answers will vary. Check for proper use of commas.

Page 84

1. September 30, 1994
2. January 1, 2012
3. May 25, 1801
4. November 19, 1940

1. Greeley, Colorado
2. Surprise, Arizona
3. New York, New York
4. San Francisco, California
5. Ottawa, Ontario
6. Beijing, China

Page 85

Answers will vary. Check for proper use of commas.

Page 86

May 7, 1996
Richmond, Virginia
April 4, 2002
Denver, Colorado
July 16, 2002
Omaha, Nebraska
July 11, 2007
October 1, 2008
Phoenix, Arizona
Juneau, Alaska

Page 88

1. Maranda,
2. Yes,
3. question, Mary,
4. Sure,
5. Frank,
6. Well,
7. Dad,
8. No,

Page 89
Answers will vary. Check for proper use of commas.

Page 90
September 4, 2008,
Estes Park,
Mike,
Yes,
Wow,

Page 92
Bond,
Sincerely,

Fixit,
Sincerely,

Bond,
Sincerely,

Page 93
Edna,
phrases,
year,
Finally,
Edna,
Wichita,
nephew,

Page 94
Answers will vary. Check for proper use of commas.

Page 96
1. "Was … missed?"
2. "Last … poodle!"
3. "This … doll,"
4. "I … tall."
5. "Would … cookie?"
6. "Look … penny!"
7. "Now I understand,"
8. "May … water?"

Page 97
"I … merry-go-round!"
"I … zebra,"
"OK! … alone,"
"The … me,"
"You're … things,"
"He … me!"
"Get … leaving!"
"Amy … zebra,"

Page 98
Answers will vary. Check for proper use of quotation marks.

Page 100
1. can
2. May
3. can
4. may
5. may
6. May
7. may
8. can
9. can
10. can

Page 101
May, may, may, can, can, can, can, can

Page 102
Answers will vary. Check for proper use of *may* and *can*.

Grammar and Punctuation Review (Downloadable Assessment—see page 2 for details)

Part A
A1. B
A2. B
A3. A
A4. C
A5. C
A6. B
A7. A
A8. A

Part B

B1. B
B2. A
B3. C
B4. C
B5. A
B6. B
B7. B
B8. A

Part C

C1. A
C2. C
C3. B
C4. C
C5. B
C6. A
C7. B
C8. C
C9. A

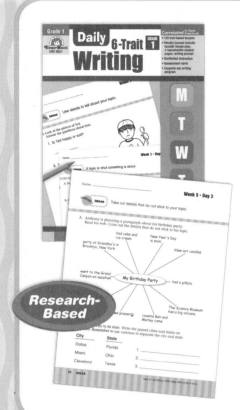

Daily 6-Trait Writing
Dynamic trait-based writing instruction that fits into any writing program!

Help your students develop trait-based writing skills using 125 daily lessons that fit into any writing program! *Daily 6-Trait Writing* is the first product to provide students in grades 1–6+ with practice and instruction on trait-based writing skills using a daily practice format. Each book in *Daily 6-Trait Writing* provides 25 weeks of direct instruction and practice in the critical skills students need to become strong and successful writers.160 reproducible pages. ***Correlated to state standards.***

Teachers love *Daily 6-Trait Writing* because it...

- *contains scaffolded lessons and activities to help target the specific skills students need most.*
- *helps students think critically about writing while evaluating and assessing various forms of writing.*
- *contains frequent, focused practice that strengthens writing fluency.*
- *provides opportunities for students to write in a variety of forms, including narrative, expository, descriptive, and persuasive.*
- *is research-based and correlated to state standards.*

Grade 1	EMC 6021–PRO	Grade 4	EMC 6024–PRO
Grade 2	EMC 6022–PRO	Grade 5	EMC 6025–PRO
Grade 3	EMC 6023–PRO	Grade 6+	EMC 6026–PRO

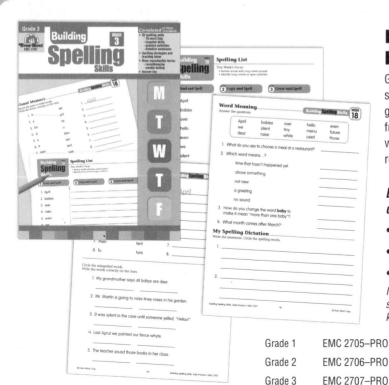

Building Spelling Skills – Daily Practice

Go beyond surface-level memorization to present students with strategies and practice for 198 to 540 grade-level spelling words! Word lists are selected from commonly used words, commonly misspelled words, and words with common elements. 160 reproducible pages. ***Correlated to state standards.***

Each book contains 30 spelling units comprised of:

- *a spelling list*
- *sentences for dictation*
- *4 reproducible student practice pages*

Includes forms for weekly testing and recordkeeping, suggestions for teaching spelling strategies, an answer key, and more!

Grade 1	EMC 2705–PRO	Grade 4	EMC 2708–PRO
Grade 2	EMC 2706–PRO	Grade 5	EMC 2709–PRO
Grade 3	EMC 2707–PRO	Grade 6+	EMC 2710–PRO